Fact Finders®

Explore the Biomes

EXPLORE THE

Ocean

by Kay Jackson

Consultant:
Dr. Sandra Mather
Professor Emerita of Geology and Astronomy
West Chester University
West Chester, Pennsylvania

Capstone *press®*

Mankato, Minnesota

Fact Finders is published by Capstone Press,
151 Good Counsel Drive, P.O. Box 669, Mankato, Minnesota 56002.
www.capstonepress.com

Library of Congress Cataloging-in-Publication Data
Jackson, Kay, 1959–
    Explore the ocean / by Kay Jackson.
    p. cm. —(Fact finders. Explore the biomes)
    Includes bibliographical references and index.
    ISBN-13: 978-0-7368-6406-0 (hardcover)
    ISBN-10: 0-7368-6406-7 (hardcover)
    ISBN-13: 978-0-7368-9629-0 (softcover pbk.)
    ISBN-10: 0-7368-9629-5 (softcover pbk.)
    1. Marine ecology—Juvenile literature. I. Title. II. Series.
QH541.5.S3J33 2007
577.7—dc22   2006004110

Summary: Discusses the plants, animals, and characteristics of the ocean biome.

Editorial Credits
Erika L. Shores, editor; Juliette Peters, designer; Tami Collins, map illustrator;
    Wanda Winch, photo researcher

Photo Credits
Corbis/Chris Hellier, 18; Lawson Wood, 14; Ralph White, 16 (tube worms)
Courtesy of Kay Jackson, 32
Creatas, 24–25
Digital Vision, 27 (clownfish)
Getty Images Inc./AFP/STF, 21; The Image Bank/Luis Castaneda Inc., 19; Stone/Jeff Rotman,
    14 (giant octopus)
James P. Rowan, 4–5
Jeff Rotman, cover (background)
Kip Evans Photography, 29
Minden Pictures/Flip Nicklin, 12–13, 27; Frans Lanting, 22–23, 23; Norbert Wu, cover
    (foreground), 15, 20; Tui De Roy, 11
Peter Arnold/Jeff Rotman, 10
Photodisc/Siede Preis, 1 (starfish), 3, 30 (shell), 8 (driftwood), 24, (sand dollar), 26 (starfish and coral)
Shutterstock/Alex James Bramwell, 19 (sardines); Alexey Bogdanov, 1, 30 (fish); Dan Bannister, 10
    (sea otter); Dennis Sabo, 6; Doxa, 28 (fish); Dwight Smith, 4; Ferenc Cegledi, 20 (dolphin); G.
    Lewis, 18 (sushi); Graham Prentice, 11 (coral); Janis Rozentals, 12 (icy sea); Soundsnaps, 6 (shark)
Tom Stack & Associates, Inc./Tom & Therisa Stack, 9
Woods Hole Oceanographic Institution, 17

Table of Contents

CHAPTER 1

The World's Ocean

Waves of ocean water crash onto a rocky shore. The salty water sprays into the air. Drops fall onto the rocks where they will be swept back out to sea. Imagine following those drops of water on a journey around the world.

The drops start their trip near the coast but soon move out to open water. They travel around continents and even under the North Pole's frozen polar ice cap. The drops drift through the world's largest **biome**, the world ocean. Five major oceans make up this huge body of water that covers 70 percent of the earth.

French grunt

Waves are made by the wind blowing across the ocean surface.

5

The Ocean Biome

A biome is made up of a large area of unique plants and animals that are adapted to their surroundings. Plants and animals in the ocean biome depend on each other for survival. Plants provide food for fish. In turn, the smaller fish are food for large ocean animals like whales and sharks.

blacktip shark

Field Note

What are the fivo major oceans?

- Antarctic Ocean
- Arctic Ocean
- Atlantic Ocean
- Indian Ocean
- Pacific Ocean

Arctic Ocean

Atlantic Ocean

Pacific Ocean

Indian Ocean

Antarctic Ocean

N
W E
S

oceans

Looking out over the waves, the ocean seems empty, but a dive below reveals an amazing world. Bright silver minnows flash by, giant whales push through the open waters, and scary creatures hide on the dark bottom. The ocean is full of life.

CHAPTER 2

Near the Shore

The ocean's coast is a busy place. Sandpipers skitter away from small waves. Little two-shelled **mollusks** dig into the wet sand. Strands of shiny seaweed pile up on the beach. Logs and branches of trees and bushes wash up on shore. Over time, ocean waves turn them into gray pieces of driftwood.

Under the smooth driftwood, two eyes on long stalks peek out. A blue crab checks to see if it's safe. It scrambles to the next bit of wood. But a wave catches the little crab. The wave drags the crab out into the shallow water at the edge of the ocean. The ocean's shallow waters are packed with all sorts of plants and animals.

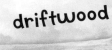

driftwood

A blue crab is just one of the many animals found in shallow ocean water.

FACT!

Blue crabs walk and swim from side to side rather than forward and backward.

Shallow Water

Kelp forests grow in the shallow water along cold, rocky coasts. Playful sea otters dive and zip between the tall kelp. They hide from hungry killer whales.

Coral reefs grow in warm, shallow areas of the ocean. Off the eastern shore of Australia is the world's largest coral reef, the Great Barrier Reef.

sea otter

Kelp lives in shallow water because it needs sunlight to grow.

Coral reefs are home to nearly one-fourth of all ocean creatures.

Millions of animals live on each coral reef. A parrotfish darts between flat fan corals and skinny pipe corals. Anemones that look like upside-down jellyfish cling to dead coral lumps. Whitetip sharks glide along the reef bottom. One hungry shark swims past the reef and out into the wide spaces of the ocean's open waters.

FACT!

Over time, the skeletons of tiny animals called coral polyps form coral reefs.

CHAPTER 3

Deep Water

Sailors call the ocean's vast open water blue water. Blue water is home to the world's largest animals, blue whales. Blue whales travel in families. Each year, blue whales cross the world ocean from the icebergs of the Arctic Circle to the icy seas of the Antarctic. These cold waters are feeding areas for blue whales.

With mouths wide open, these warm-blooded giants suck in gallons of water. Bonelike structures in their mouths filter out tons of tiny animals called krill. The whales swim over the deepest parts of the ocean.

icy Antarctic sea

One blue whale can weigh
as much as 100 tons
(91 metric tons).

Shrimp have 10 legs and 10 smaller legs called swimmerets used for swimming.

The Ocean Floor

Life on the ocean floor is much different from life near the sunny surface. A giant octopus looks through the dark water. A vampire squid darts by. Bits of dead plants and animals float down like snow. Plants can't grow in the darkness so these small pieces are food for animals on the ocean floor. A shrimp snatches up a food speck.

The viperfish is another ocean animal suited for life near the dark ocean floor. Viperfish have organs on their bodies that make light. The spots of light attract small fish to swim near the viperfish. With a quick snap of its jaws, the viperfish can snag a tasty meal.

giant octopus

CHAPTER 4

People and the Ocean

In recent years, people have come to explore the deep ocean. The motors on the small **submersible**, ALVIN, slowly turn it around. Three scientists look out ALVIN's small windows. As ALVIN turns, black smoke pours from tall chimneys made of **minerals** on the ocean floor.

The black smoke is a mix of very hot water and minerals. The mix rises out of chimneys that scientists call black smokers. Giant red and white tube worms live around the smokers' edges. Spider crabs scramble through the worms. ALVIN's cameras snap pictures of the strange creatures before returning to the ocean surface.

tube worms

Scientists study the deepest areas of the ocean up-close in a submersible.

Food from the Ocean

People don't just explore the ocean, they depend on it for food. Bright green seaweed grows in oceans around the world. People wrap rice and fish in seaweed to make sushi. Seaweed can also be cooked in soups and sauces.

sushi

Seaweed farmers harvest the dark green plant from shallow ocean water.

Every day, commercial fishers take tons of fish from the ocean.

sardines

Huge fishing boats drag miles-long nets behind them. Each month, thousands of fish are caught in these nets. People around the world eat tuna, swordfish, sardines, and many other kinds of ocean fish.

Once it is trapped in a fishing net, a sea turtle struggles to stay alive.

Threats to the Ocean

Companies that take fish from the ocean accidentally trap turtles and other ocean animals in their nets. Some kinds of seals, dolphins, and sea turtles are endangered because so many of these animals die in fishing nets every year.

bottlenose dolphin

20

Pollution also threatens the ocean and its creatures. When oil spills from giant tanker ships, it coats sea birds and seals. Then these animals can't fly or swim. Garbage left on beaches is also a threat to ocean animals. Ocean animals sometimes eat the garbage and die.

People work to clean up a massive oil spill off the coast of Spain.

Endangered Green Turtles

Green turtles feel the effects of people's actions on both the beach and the ocean. Under a bright moon, waves wash up on the white sands of a Florida beach. Female green turtles come to lay their eggs in the warm sands. In a few months, tiny green turtles cover the beach. The hatchlings scramble to the water.

Many hatchlings never make it to the ocean. Seabirds and crabs often eat the turtles.

The tiny turtles that reach the Atlantic Ocean continue to grow. They swim many miles before returning to the turtle beach. But each year fewer green turtles come back to the beach where they hatched.

The green turtle is an endangered animal. People hunt the turtle for its meat and skin. Homes built on turtle beaches destroy their nesting grounds. Without the help of people, turtles and other ocean animals might disappear forever.

Protecting the Ocean

Many people want to protect the ocean. Conservation groups work to keep beaches clean and to protect endangered ocean animals. These groups teach people about why the ocean is important.

Countries also work together to protect the ocean. Countries pass laws that make it illegal to dump garbage and chemicals into the ocean. They sometimes sign **treaties** to stop whaling and overfishing.

Some governments also promise to protect seals, otters, and turtles from hunters. Working together, people can keep the ocean safe for the millions of plants and animals that live there.

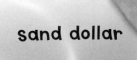

sand dollar

Picking up trash on ocean beaches is one way to protect ocean animals.

CHAPTER 5

Ocean Field Guide

Oceans:

Antarctic Ocean, Arctic Ocean, Atlantic Ocean, Indian Ocean, Pacific Ocean

OCEAN TEMPERATURES:

At the North Pole and the South Pole, the ocean's surface temperature is about 28 degrees Fahrenheit (minus 2 degrees Celsius). In areas where the seasons change, ocean water is colder in winter and warmer in summer.

Question:

What are some ways you can help protect the ocean and its plants and animals?

ANIMALS:

Crabs: blue crabs, king crabs, rock crabs, spider crabs

Deep ocean animals: dragonfish, eels, fangtooth fish, giant squids, shrimp, vampire squids, viperfish

Reef animals: clownfish, mantis shrimp, rays, sharks, starfish

Whales: beluga whales, blue whales, bowhead whales, gray whales, humpback whales, killer whales

PLANTS:

dinoflagellates, kelp, phytoplankton, seaweed, turtle grass

Ocean products: fish, seaweed, oil found below the ocean floor

CHAPTER 6

A Scientist at Work

As a little girl, Dr. Sylvia Earle wanted to swim like a dolphin. When she grew up, Earle made her dream come true by becoming an oceanographer. As an ocean scientist, she swam with whales in Hawaii, studied algae in the Gulf of Mexico, and explored coral reefs in the Indian Ocean.

To learn about the deep ocean, Earle traveled 1,250 feet (381 meters) below the ocean surface in a special suit. To dive even deeper, Earle designed a deep sea submersible.

To share her love and knowledge of the ocean, Earle writes children's books about its amazing creatures. She wants children to love the ocean as much as she does.

GLOSSARY

biome (BUY-ome)—an area with a particular type of climate, and certain plants and animals that live there

mineral (MIN-ur-uhl)—a solid found in nature that is not made by people, animals, or plants; minerals can be found on earth's surface or underground.

mollusk (MOL-uhsk)—an animal with a soft body and no spine

pollution (puh-LOO-shuhn)—harmful materials that damage the air, water, and soil

submersible (suhb-MURS-uh-buhl)—a small underwater craft powered by motors

treaty (TREE-tee)—an official agreement between two or more groups or countries

INTERNET SITES

FactHound offers a safe, fun way to find Internet sites related to this book. All of the sites on FactHound have been researched by our staff.

Here's how:

1. Visit *www.facthound.com*

2. Choose your grade level.

3. Type in this book ID **0736864067** for age-appropriate sites. You may also browse subjects by clicking on letters, or by clicking on pictures and words.

4. Click on the **Fetch It** button.

FactHound will fetch the best sites for you!

READ MORE

Green, Jen. *Saving Oceans and Wetlands.* Precious Earth. North Mankato, Minn.: Chrysalis Education, 2004.

Johnson, Rebecca L. *Journey into the Ocean.* Biomes of North America. Minneapolis: Carolrhoda Books, 2004.

Pyers, Greg. *Ocean Explorer.* Habitat Explorer. Chicago: Raintree, 2005.

INDEX

ABOUT THE AUTHOR

Kay Jackson

Kay Jackson writes nonfiction books for children. Kay grew up near the Gulf of Mexico. Since then, she's paddled off the coast of California, built sandcastles on beaches in West Africa, and snorkeled Florida's coral reefs. Kay and her husband are building an ocean-going boat. Soon, they'll sail about the world. For now, Kay lives and writes in Tulsa, Oklahoma, close to the last bit of North America's tallgrass prairie.